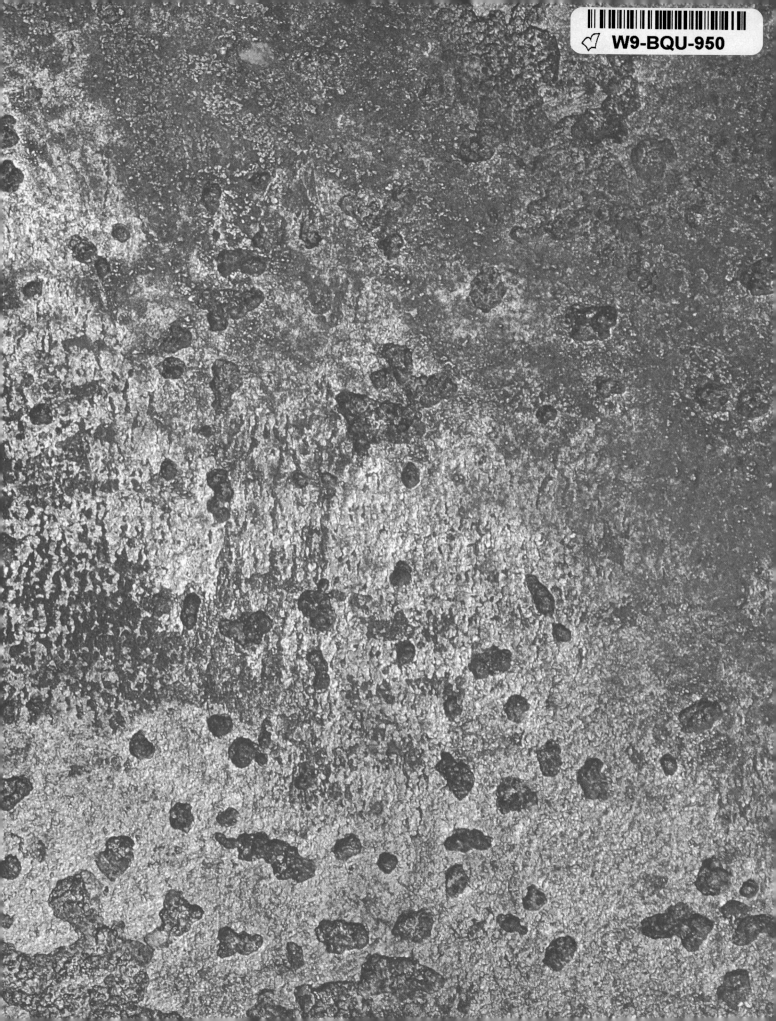

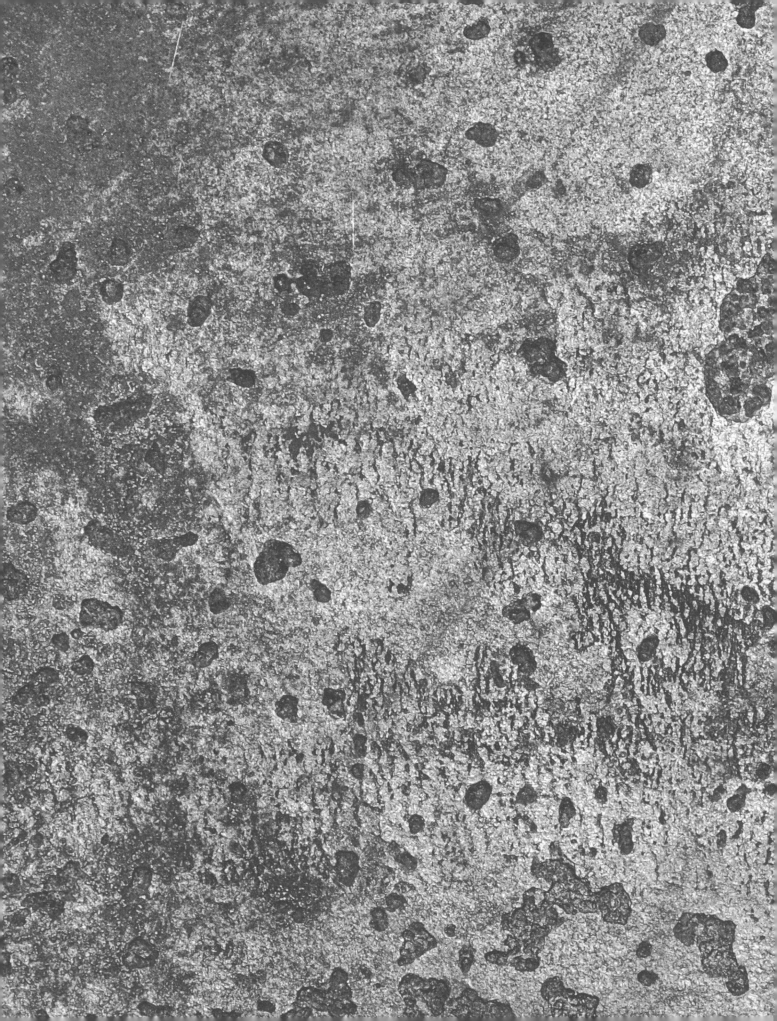

First published in 2015 by Motorbooks, an imprint of Quarto Publishing Group USA Inc.,
400 First Avenue North, Suite 400, Minneapolis, MN 55401 USA

Motorbooks titles are also available at discounts in bulk quantity for industrial or sales-promotional use. For details write to Special Sales Manager at Quarto Publishing Group USA Inc., 400 First Avenue North, Suite 400, Minneapolis, MN 55401 USA.

To find out more about our books, visit us online at www.motorbooks.com.

ISBN: 978-0-7603-4807-9

Library of Congress Cataloging-in-Publication Data

Brutt, Ryan, 1983-
  Amazing barn finds and roadside relics : musty Mustangs, forgotten Fords, hidden Hudsons, and other lost automotive gems / Ryan Brutt.
      pages cm
  Summary: "Ryan Brutt's Amazing Barn Finds and Roadside Relics is a cross-country photographic account of some of the most remarkable abandoned car "graveyards" and abandoned barns and garages around, and the forlorn (and often rare) vehicles found within"-- Provided by publisher.
    ISBN 978-0-7603-4807-9 (hardback)
  1. Automobile graveyards--United States--Pictorial works. I. Title.
  TD795.4.B78 2015
  629.2220973--dc23
                                    2015018809

Acquisitions Editor: Zack Miller
Project Manager: Jordan Wiklund
Art Director: Cindy Samargia Laun
Cover Design: Simon Larkin
Book Design and Layout: Simon Larkin

Printed in China

10 9 8 7 6 5 4 3 2 1

AMAZING
BARN
FINDS
AND ROADSIDE RELICS

MUSTY MUSTANGS,
HIDDEN HUDSONS,
FORGOTTEN FORDS,
and other lost
automotive gems

RYAN BRUTT

CONTENTS

INTRODUCTION

This all started because of a story and a radio. In 1970, my father bought a new Hemi 'Cuda. He told me stories about how he used to race it, and when he blew up the engine, he threw in another big-block, riveted the shaker bubble to the hood, and away he rumbled once more.

Thirty years later, I was driving a beat-up 1990 Ford Taurus station wagon as my first car. I wasn't into cars then. But someone else was into my car—someone really wanted the radio and stole the tape deck. Afterward, Dad arranged for a friend to put a CD player into the car for cheap. At the shop where the wagon was getting the radio, I spied something between the two work bays. It was a car underneath a ton of general junk from around the shop—upholstery

materials, tools, car parts, and more. I think there was even a hard top for a Corvette on it. Underneath it all, though, was something special, even now—a 1971 Plymouth 'Cuda.

Finding that car in that shape was the spark I needed. The car was cool, with the cheese grater grille, the gilled side fenders, the unique rear taillights. It looked like nothing on the road. That was the moment that changed my life. I was hooked on muscle cars.

I loved the thrill that something this cool could be tucked away, hidden like a lost Incan temple in the Amazon or a ship at rest at the bottom of the sea. And once I found one, I asked around and found more. And more. And more. It didn't stop.

Eventually, I started going on expeditions to find as much American automotive memorabilia as possible. I would beat the ground and drive around aimlessly, no real destination in mind, but I'd usually find something—something cool,

more often than not. A GTO, or maybe a C3 Corvette. You never know what you are going to uncover. Some of my best finds—like that first 1971 'Cuda—were completely by accident, and others I have been given leads to. But you just don't know what is out there.

People always say, "There are no more hidden cars—they've all been found!"

I intend to prove them wrong.

Ryan Brutt

CHAPTER 1:
NOT FOR SALE

You're driving through the countryside and you catch something out of the corner of your eye: The taillights of an old car peeking from beneath a tarp. You back up and find the driveway. Maybe the car is something really great. You want to take a look.

You pull up to the house and do the polite thing by knocking on the door. You wait a few moments and then the owner swings the door open and looks at you. He's a crusty guy, and he knows why you're here. He's been through this before.

He says, "It's not for sale."

And that's that.

While I attended college, I found this 1970 Chevelle SS sitting next to a home, and there it sat the entire time I was at school. I went back after nearly a decade and the car hadn't moved an inch.

This was the first hidden car I ever discovered, a 1971 Plymouth 'Cuda sitting in a car stereo shop in Chicago. I was having a radio installed in my daily driver and the 'Cuda was sitting between the two major work areas. It sat in the same spot for over a decade.

Driving to a nearby quarry, I looked just off the road and saw this car sitting in the old barn. This 1967 Plymouth Satellite had been there for over a decade, sidelined because of a bad brake line. The car never moved from that spot in the entire time I lived in the area.

My friend informed me about this car, a 1970 Plymouth Barracuda. This car was in the garage since 1977, sidelined for long-forgotten reasons. The corner of the garage where the car sat had not been touched since the car was parked in the corner. Everything was untouched, as it was in 1977.

Shooting a yard in Iowa, this poor neglected Mustang was rotting outside—a 1966 Mustang GT with a 289 hi-po V-8.

This 1969 Dodge Super Bee was supposedly in an accident involving a concrete wall. Afterwards the owner parted it out, but left the hulk in the field for the cows to use as a rubbing post.

Out west is a landmark—the Cadillac by the barn. I had heard stories and seen pictures of it but never seen it in person until this point. I just happened to find it while on a different expedition, and the weather was perfect for the shot.

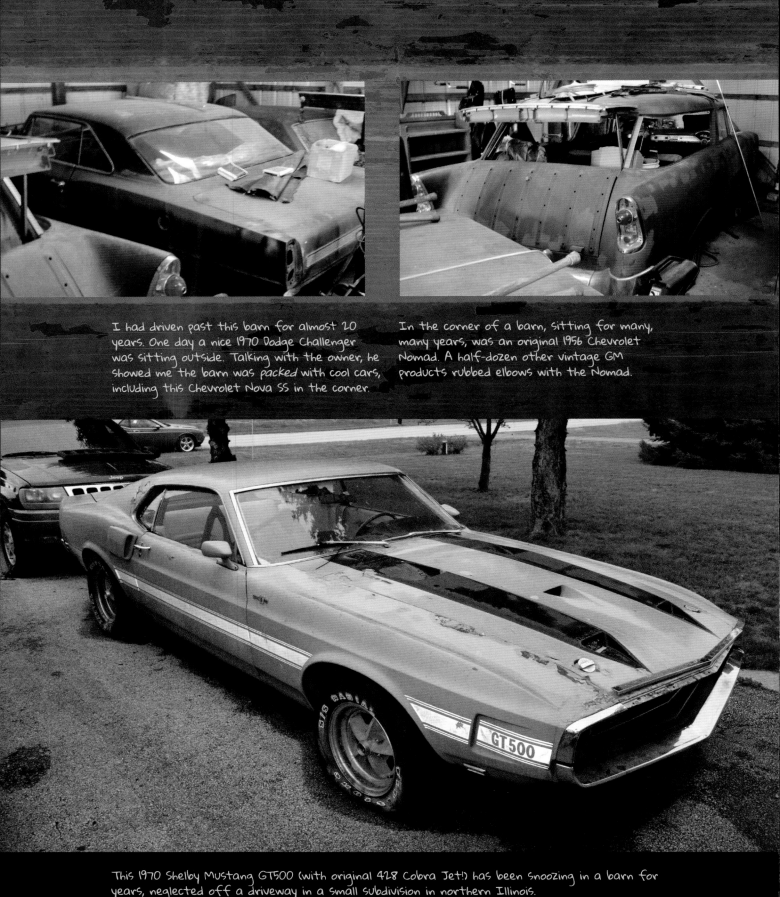

I had driven past this barn for almost 20 years. One day a nice 1970 Dodge Challenger was sitting outside. Talking with the owner, he showed me the barn was *packed* with cool cars, including this Chevrolet Nova SS in the corner.

In the corner of a barn, sitting for many, many years, was an original 1956 Chevrolet Nomad. A half-dozen other vintage GM products rubbed elbows with the Nomad.

This 1970 Shelby Mustang GT500 (with original 428 Cobra Jet!) has been snoozing in a barn for years, neglected off a driveway in a small subdivision in northern Illinois.

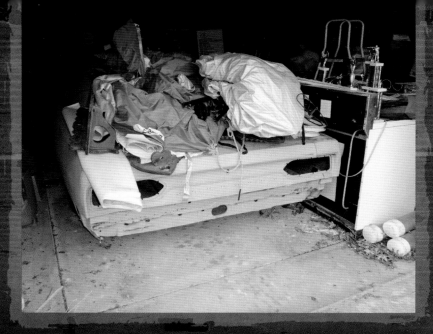

Showing up at a friend's house, he unburied his 1970 Plymouth Road Runner just enough to get a handful of pictures. The car has been buried in the garage for years.

Over the years, I have been in that situation many times. The truth is that some collectible cars will never be for sale. You come across them sitting in junkyards, or resting in a grove of trees in somebody's backyard. You look at the car and all you can do is shake your head. It's sad to think of some old gem rotting away, forgotten. When you drive off, you hope that someday the car will be saved.

Every car has a history, and even the seemingly forgotten ones didn't get stashed away by accident. There's always a reason. Sentiment can have a lot to do with it. The car may have been somebody's first ride, or the one the owner drove on romantic dates long ago. Perhaps the car belonged to a son who went off to war and never came home again.

My friend drove me around showing me all sorts of crazy cars sitting in fields and junkyards. This 1967 LeMans Convertible sat neglected in the field for decades, slowly rusting to the ground.

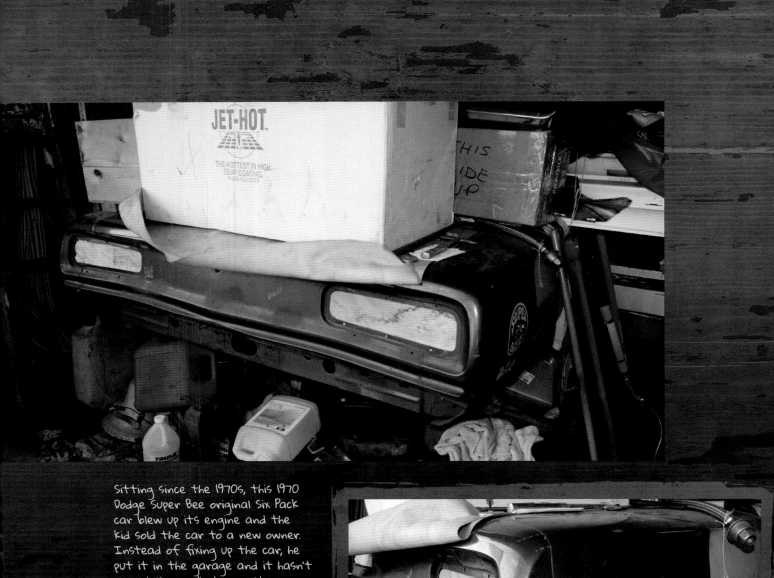

Sitting since the 1970s, this 1970 Dodge Super Bee original Six Pack car blew up its engine and the kid sold the car to a new owner. Instead of fixing up the car, he put it in the garage and it hasn't moved since. What a waste.

As you might imagine, family and time are common reasons why particular cars seem doomed to rot away. Maybe the owner had once fussed over it, and then became preoccupied with the responsibilities of a growing family. The years rolled on, and the car sat and sat. Many owners have good intentions, and tell themselves that, one day, they will grab their tools and start a restoration of the car they loved.

Outsiders—neighbors, distant relatives, and garden-variety busybodies—may be jealous that the owner has an interesting old car and they don't. They say the person is a hoarder, with a mental

Mopar guys almost always have a car or two hanging around. This gentleman actively bought and sold Mopar parts, and had this real A12 6 bbl Road Runner tucked away in the corner of his barn. Very cool.

disorder that prevents the person from letting the car go. Well, we should be thankful that the cars have been saved. Most vintage muscle cars, for instance, were driven hard and eventually made their way to the crusher. They're gone. But the select few that sit in backyards and dusty garages are survivors. We hope to see them resurrected one day, and brought back to their original glory.

On the other hand, some owners of old, unrestored classics keep them in plain sight because they like the attention. They know they're not going to sell, but they get a kick out of chatting with would-be buyers, and seeing the car lust in their eyes. The car makes owners of this sort feel special. Without the car, what else do they have? So the car sits, and people keep coming to the door. Inevitably, the visitors go away disappointed.

You always have to keep your eyes open. Traveling through Wisconsin, I came across a gentleman who had a wide variety of Chevrolet products sitting around his property. One of the cooler cars was a 1967 Chevelle SS 396 sitting out back in the weeds.

It is always a good idea to ask your friends what they have lying around. One day my friend mentioned his family had a 1928 Model A Town Sedan sitting in the barn. They have had the car in the family for many generations and hope someday to restore the car to its former glory.

A 1970 Plymouth 'Cuda 340 sits in the corner of a garage, forlorn for many years and waiting for the day that its owner starts turning wrenches on her again. Thankfully this antique has been stored in a nice garage for little more than 20 years.

Family obligations are the usual reason that a car has sat for so long. This 1967 Pontiac GTO suffered the same fate as many other muscle cars—the owner got busy with life and had to put away the car for a rainy day. Some do get them out again, while others let them rot away to nothing.

This relic was originally bought new by the current owner's grandmother. She had walked into the local Dodge dealer to buy a new Polara or Monaco, but fell in love with the Burnt Orange 70 Charger. She bought it on the spot, and it has been in the family ever since.

The reason I get close looks at a lot of amazing old cars is that I don't walk up and ask if I can buy them. Instead, I let the owner know that I've come to find out about the car's history. How long have you had it? Was it something special in your life? You've made a point to hang onto it. Can you tell me why?

I really want to know.

Owners are usually happy to show the car and share their stories. At the end, I always ask them to let me know if they ever decide to sell. Perhaps we could work something out.

If they decide to do a restoration, I can point them to parts and useful information. Everyone is happy, though I suppose the old cars will not be completely happy until they receive the attention they need.

Here lies a 1968 Pontiac GTO convertible, a 400-ci V-8 car with a 4-speed, originally painted a nice shade of red. The owner had it parked among a bunch of other vehicles on the property and plans to fix it up someday soon.

The 1970s and '80s were the height of the van craze. Customized vans could be seen on the covers of many magazines, and this Dodge Street Van would have been right there in the thick of it. It remains as an intriguing time capsule of another era.

An adventure is around every corner when you are with friends. This 1972 Plymouth Satellite Sebring Plus was well off the beaten path, but my friend had seen it while cruising the back roads. We were lucky to find it again.

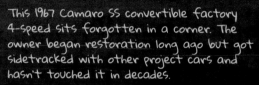

This 1967 Camaro SS convertible factory 4-speed sits forgotten in a corner. The owner began restoration long ago but got sidetracked with other project cars and hasn't touched it in decades.

Traveling the back roads is the best way to find interesting vehicles. This Oldsmobile Cutlass was just off a gravel road, and has been there for decades. The license plate is from 1976!

I shot this 1970 Dodge Super Bee a few years ago when it was in a lean-to next to a barn. The owner rolled it out to clean the area, and there it sat ever since. That's a real Hemi Orange car!

Tucked away safely in an old barn, this 1969 Dodge Super Bee Six Pack car is extremely clean.

It is all about who you know. For over a year I played Telephone with a local club member about a Camaro that he had tucked away. I finally got to meet the guy—his nickname is Monk—and saw that the Camaro was a 1969 Z/28 with a 4-speed. It's been sitting since the '80s.

A relic from the '70s, this 1970 Plymouth 340 'Cuda was tucked safely away in the owner's mother's lakeside home in the early '80s and never un-tucked. Still sitting in the same location, the only thing that changes is the buildup of dust over time.

1964 was the 50th anniversary of automaker Dodge, so to commemorate it they manufactured several special editions of their vehicles. This 1964 Dodge Polara convertible with the 50th Anniversary package has been sitting for years.

To make more room, a loft was built over this 1968 Chevrolet Camaro RS/SS 350. The current owner bought it after a friend passed on the opportunity, believing it to be too rough. Since the new owner has a variety of other GM muscle projects in the wings, he stuck it in the corner for a rainy day.

This is one of those cars you hear about in myth and legends. My friend is an A-body Mopar expert (Dodge Darts, Demons, Dart Sports, Plymouth Valiant, Dusters, etc.) and hunted most of his life for the holy grail of nearly any muscle car make. Tucked away in a barn he found a 1968 Hemi SS Dart, bought it on the spot, and then stuck it in his barn for a rainy day.

BEER,
ROMANCE,
AND THE 'GTX

A thoughtful reader of the Auto Archaeology column I do for *Hot Rod* tipped me that his friend had a rare 1970 Plymouth GTX, one of just 1,471 made. The car was stored in a building not far from the reader's home. I expressed interest, so the reader took me to his friend and introduced me to the car.

The property was in the middle of Indiana. We met the owner and then walked around to the barn where the car was safely tucked away. The barn was jammed full of stuff. We had to squeeze around lawn-care equipment and old furniture. The owner was behind us, and just as we got to the car, he threw the barn door wide open. Light came in, and we could see what he had.

It was a '70 GTX, all right. It had come off the line with a 440-cid V-8 and a 4-speed transmission. The owner blew up the engine sometime in the '70s and handed it to a friend for a rebuild. Weeks turned into months, and the rebuilt engine never materialized. When the owner finally asked his pal about the wait, the guy admitted that he'd traded the engine for beer! There are plenty of things a reasonable man might give up for beer—money, scrap metal, certain members of his extended family—but a friend's engine shouldn't be one of them!

Ever since the 440 went missing, the car has been sitting, shuffled from one storage space to another. At one point the owner threw a 383 into the engine compartment but never took the final steps that would have made the GTX a running, driving car.

I talked with the owner for a while and shot some pictures. As usual, the why question began to bubble in my brain. Why hang on to the thing? The owner confided that, well, he was pretty sure his son had been conceived in the back seat.

That seemed a good enough reason to keep the old GTX around.

LUCKY DOG

I had enjoyed traveling across North Carolina for a few days, but I needed to get ready for the *Hot Rod* Power Tour 2014. I wanted to relax before I got into a six-day, seven-city drive across multiple states. I was about to head out when a local friend told me his father had a lead on something I'd be interested in. We met up with Dad and then all three of us drove to a shop surrounded by storage barns and farmland. The owner took us around back. As a couple of guard terriers barked loudly, the owner let us look at a few cars sitting around in the open. He had a 1969 GTO and a rare electric '56 Plymouth Fury toy car. A '71 340 Duster was interesting, but the coolest item was a 1971 Ford Mustang Mach 1. The only odd thing about any of it was that one of the terriers stared at the Mach 1, barking like crazy.

The owner took us into the barn, where he kept his better cars. There was a 1973 Road Runner with a 340 and a '68 Dodge Dart GTS with a 340. The farther into the barn we got, the cooler the cars became. There was a 1971 Dodge Challenger ragtop, a '71 Challenger R/T with a 383, and a '67 Plymouth GTX 440. I could hardly believe it. Tucked out of sight in this barn were some of the best muscle cars in the world. It was incredible.

Back outside we saw even more vintage muscle. A '71 Challenger R/T with the rare wide hood molding sat in the weeds, where a tree had grown up through the engine compartment. Sitting next to it was a '70 Barracuda.

Then there was the shed, where the owner had squirreled away a 1964 GTO with a 389 and tri-power; a 1971 Boss 351 Mustang; and a '67 Barracuda. There was even a 1978 or '79 Dodge Li'l Red Express Truck.

We came back from the shed and found the terrier still barking at the Mach 1. The dog suddenly darted forward and came out with a poisonous snake in its jaws. The moment before the dog killed the snake, the snake bit the dog. The owner rushed his dog to an emergency vet for treatment with anti-venom. The pup survived.

You just never know how things are going to end up on these adventures.

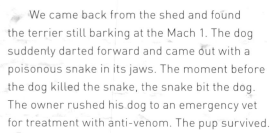

A FOREST
IN NORTH CAROLINA

A few years back, my best friend moved from Chicago to North Carolina. When he was looking at houses, he came across something incredible: a field packed with mostly prewar Fords. My friend isn't an old-car guy, so he waited for me to come visit before checking out the collection.

I flew out and the two of us headed to the site. My friend thought we would just cruise by and grab a picture or two; I had other ideas. The place was private property. We pulled into the driveway and met the owner, who happened to be outside. He was talkative and allowed us full access to his yard.

Closest to the drive was a row of old, open tractor sheds. Each bay held at least one car, and every car had stuff piled every which way on top of it. A lot of nifty petroliana was lying around, too, from old oil can advertising racks to complete gas pumps. Car stuff was everywhere.

As I walked, I couldn't believe how many vintage cars were scattered around the property. Some had sat for so long that full-size trees had grown through their bodies or engine compartments, making them part of the scenery. Most of the cars were Fords dating from the 1930s to the early 60s, everything from a flathead 4-banger to a 390 big block. They had been there a long time but, all things considered, were not in terrible shape.

Here and there amidst the literal forest of cars were a few Plymouths, Pontiacs, and other makes. A 50s-era DeSoto still had its original, first-generation Hemi.

We ate up an entire afternoon chatting with the owner and shooting everything. I thanked him for letting us walk around the place. He said he was happy to see young people who appreciated the collection he had put together over decades. It was a part of him.

MUSCLE MEETS THE
INSURANCE
MAN

The universe works in funny ways. I was at a small-town car show in southern Wisconsin when an extremely rare 1968 Dodge Charger R/T drove in. This was an original 426 Hemi, the King Kong of engines, the "elephant" beloved by collectors. All the power went through a 4-speed manual transmission. I talked with the owner, and told him that I shoot at car shows, junkyards, and other places. He said he had a few other Mopars I might like to see.

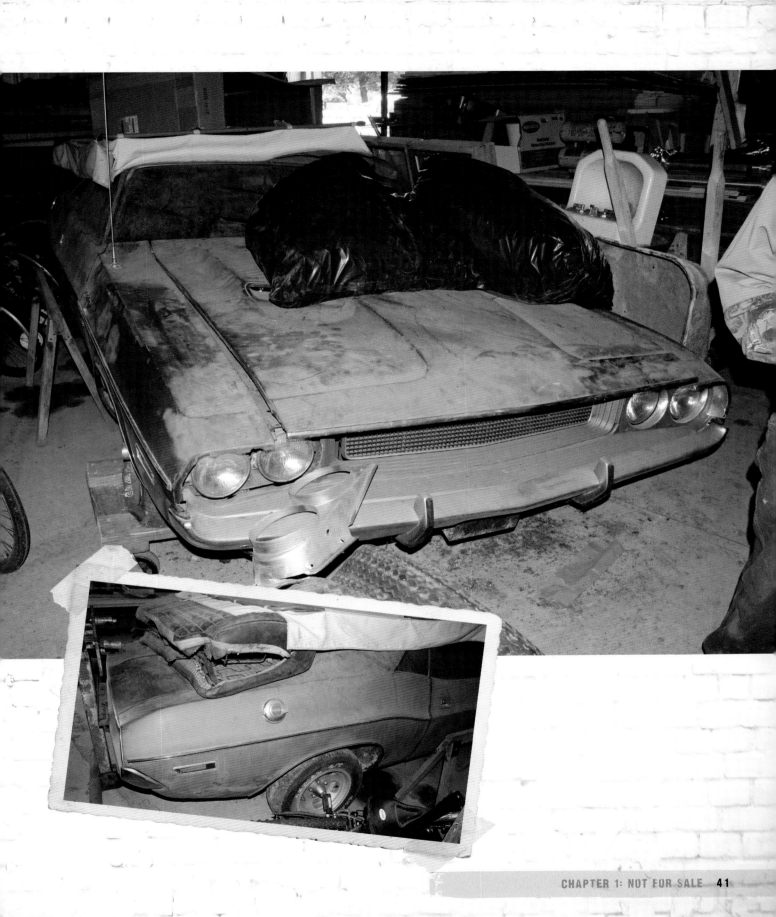

He was happy to show off the Hemi as we drove in it to the center of town. Over the years, I had gone past the unassuming old steel-sided barn hundreds of times. I would occasionally wonder what was behind those doors. The Hemi man opened them a crack so I could see a pair of Dodge Challengers.

One was a rare 1970 SE; the other was a '72. The '70 was unique because, although it had a 383-cid V-8 big block and an upgraded interior, it was not an R/T. Most buyers of the day that wanted the big block ordered the R/T. But *smart* buyers knew that in order to get around high insurance rates, you ordered the big motor in a Challenger model slotted below the R/T. Those buyers drove off with a

big-block Challenger that had everything an R/T had, without it being a high-premium R/T. Pretty smart!

The '72 looked like a solid project. It had no engine, but rolled without issue and had no significant rust. Coming from an area where metal rusted away after just a few years, the '72 was a very nice example.

Both Challengers had sat for years and years. The owner, a one-time employee of the local Dodge/Plymouth/Chrysler dealership, had a longtime affinity for Mopar product. He had a hoard of parts and kept a '67 Chrysler Newport for tinkering.

But for the time being, he was happy to play around with his Hemi Charger.

THE KID
HAD A BISCAYNE

In 1961, a 16-year-old boy and his mother walked into Fencl-Bogan Chevrolet in Oak Park, Illinois, and ordered a race car. Well, what they ordered would eventually become a race car. It was a 1962 Chevy Biscayne with a 350-bhp, 348-cid V-8 mated to a 4-speed transmission. The young man was too young to have a car in his name, so his mom signed off on the specifications and the sale.

Through the years, the young man made the car faster and faster, and ran it under the name *The Runaway*. It was so fast, it appeared on covers of programs for the infamous Chicago Amphitheater Indoor Drag Races. The kid won many races. He was on a roll when he enlisted in the 101st Airborne.

He was 20 when he got out in 1964, and took a job at Chicago's performance-oriented Nickey Chevrolet. The dealership was famed for its

backwards "K" and for performance hop-ups that put Nickey in the same class as Yenko and Chicago's Mr. Norm.

Fast forward to 1968, when the young man wanted a change of perspective and became a Chicago cop. He was with the department for decades, and through it all he kept *The Runaway*, the race car his mother helped him buy, tucked safely away in storage. He began to restore the car in the '80s, but some people working on it with him

STOCK CLASS

B/SS

QUARTER MILE CLUB
NATIONAL

stole parts and his money. The experience soured his mood toward *The Runaway*, so he put the car in the corner and let it collect dust for a long time.

I was a member of a local car club, the Chicago Gearheads, and I'd been hearing about this car for years. Eventually I got together with the owner, who arranged for me to see the big Biscayne. When I came to photograph the car, the man and his wife were at work in the garage, clearing away years of boxes and lawn furniture that had buried the Chevy over the years.

I immediately told them to stop what they were doing, that I wanted to shoot the car just as it was found. They answered that unless they cleaned up at least a little, I would never have known a car was there at all.

The Biscayne was dirty but still looked intimidating. I shot it and then talked some more with the owner. As I was getting ready to leave, the gentleman's wife thanked me for coming by. In all the years of her marriage, she had never seen the car so clean!

CHAPTER 2:
RODE HARD, PUT AWAY WET

I've driven around the country for years, investigating "barn finds," "garage finds," what have you. Inevitably, there is another car to be discovered, and another one after that. It might be a '32 Ford hot rod or a 1970 Hemi 'Cuda. You never know what you're going to find—and I've found a little bit of it all! But a single thread connects these discoveries: the cars were not recent additions to the fabric of the owners' lives. Usually, the people have owned the cars for decades. Best of all is that there is always a story that explains the "why" of their long ownership of that resting hot rod or 'Cuda.

Routinely I drive into Wisconsin where my family has a summer home. I try to take a different route each time heading up there. On one of my trips, I saw a Quonset hut that had a handful of old cars sitting out front. Pulling in and talking with the owner, he showed me his 1969 Dodge Super Bee—an original 383 big-block—that he has stored on a lift for years.

I had heard from a reader of my *Hot Rod* magazine column that his brother-in-law had a few interesting cars hidden in a barn. I'm not one to pass up old cars in a barn, so I headed out and shot an original 4-speed 1968 Camaro SS 396 convertible as well as a 1960 MGA. They had both been sitting since the early 1980s.

I let people know that I'm curious, and the approach has allowed me to see many incredible vehicles that are usually shielded from strangers' eyes. I have learned that people don't respond well to unsolicited offers to buy a car. As we have already seen in this book, people will open up when they understand that the visit is about a story, rather than a transfer of title.

Stories. Think back to the time when these cars were new. All those years ago, a car meant freedom. You got your driver's license and suddenly nothing stood in your way. You had crossed a threshold separating the few miles available to you on your bicycle from the ability to go anywhere. If you wanted to drive across the country, you could do that. If you had to go to the store for milk, you could do that, too.

In 2013 I traveled Route 66, finding cool old Americana along the way. While exploring a small town, I found this 1970 Plymouth GTX in a repair shop in Texas. A 440, this specimen was owned by the shop owner's brother. The shop owner gladly stored it for his brother until he was ready to work on the car again.

There is a gentleman in the northeast part of the country who has a ton of vintage vehicles hanging around. This 1955 Dodge Royal Lancer was driven for a short period of time, then tucked away behind this bus for a future project.

This 1969 Plymouth Barracuda was no lowly slant-six model, but a rare big-block, and it even runs. It had been put away because of other obligations, and now sits among the hot rods.

Not something you see very often. This 1962 Plymouth Fury was not one of the rare factory Max Wedge race cars of the day, but a good tribute. Once a running, driving car, it has sat for years in the corner of the barn.

If you wanted to have a drag car, this was one of the best options. This 1965 Dodge Coronet was a post car, making it lighter and stronger for racing. This '65 still had its original 1970s-inspired paint job on it, and looked like it could be cleaned up and taken out to the drag strip any time!

One of the hottest "small" cars of the Muscle Car wars was the Dodge Demon, produced for only two years under that name. It could be built with a hot 340-ci small-block V-8. This is an original 340 Demon, sitting in the barn and waiting someday to be brought back out into

The same gentleman had a few barns scattered around his property. This 1947 Dodge Business Coupe was driven into the barn years ago and hasn't been out since. Like many of the others, it looks like it could be brought back to life with little work.

Sitting on a two-post lift for who knows how long, this 1966 Dodge Charger dangles in the air. It had been there so long that it would be a serious chore to move all the parts underneath to even be able to lower the car. But at least the mice can't get to it!

Cars had an almost mythic presence in people's lives, and for many guys and girls, cars are what defined them. It didn't matter what sort of car—only that the young owner was the car and the car was the owner. You still hear stories about people recalled as "Frankie with the 'Vette" or "Nick with the Charger." Some of the cars evolved into myth and legend. To the people that hung on to their cars for many years, the machines were tangible parts of their pasts, a link they never lost.

Usually, though, people marry and find jobs. The hot rod is relegated to the garage. It may come out for the occasional car show, or perhaps for a few runs at the track. Generally, more important things come up and hobbies are pushed further away from the centers of our lives. Eventually, a car might become a shelf to store cans of paint and tools. But the car still exists. It isn't gone. It hasn't been lost to time. Sitting there in the garage or in the barn, it is a direct link to an earlier, different time, back before kids and the mortgage.

A old hot-rodded 1966 Dodge Coronet sits among its brothers in the barn. A well-warmed-over 440 sits between the fender wells, and an air cleaner sits above the hood. This thing must have been a terror on the roads.

Here is the quintessential '50s-era hot-rodded vehicle. This late-'50s Dodge features scallops, a variety of colors, and even a custom grille. You couldn't miss this thing going down the road!

In a nearly closed junkyard in Wisconsin there was one barn left that had a handful of cars. This Rambler from AMC was tucked in the back, protecting the barn and all its dusty memories.

Something you don't see every day—a Nash Metropolitan, driven into the barn of an old junkyard years ago. It hasn't been touched since, and though it needs a bit of work, the car is nearly stock and ready for restoration.

When going through an old barn in an old junkyard, you don't expect to find a very rare electric vehicle. Yet there it was—a Bradley GTE ELE. An early attempt to make an electric car, I don't know what sidelined it here. But it looks complete.

Right by the doors of the barn sat a 1966 Dodge Dart GT. The owner of the yard said it ran and drove, though who knows how long ago that was. But the tires were still full of air, and it looked like it could be driven out of there if needed.

In the middle of this garage sat a 1970 Chevelle SS 396 beneath a car cover. This was the daily driver for the family until someone kicked a large dent in the door at a theme park in Florida. It has basically been sitting ever since. It's probably worth more than a trip to Orlando.

In my travels, I listen to the story of each car, and how a once-prized possession came to sit for 20 or 30 years. You might think that a few stories are repeated over and over: *My son grew up and moved away. The car was too expensive to fool with. I guess I just didn't have the time anymore.* And there are stories like those. Most of the tales, though, revolve around the car's status as a significant part of the owner's past. Even as the world spins and changes, an owner can still walk to the garage to look at that precious piece of personal history. That person is lucky.

It's great to see young kids get into cars. This 1968 Dodge Super Bee was saved from the crusher by a young muscle car fan. It had been sitting for a long time, but was a nice car when it was put away.

Another car that was about to be crushed after being put away a decade or more ago. A 1969 Plymouth Road Runner sits forlorn in a field where it was dropped after being saved from the scrapper.

Here an old Ford Coupe sits in the corner, long ago driven into this storage space that was once a department store. It's been sitting so long the bias ply tires have completely degraded.

It's great to have an audience who enjoys reading my column in *Hot Rod* magazine. A reader introduced me to this gentleman, who had a rather unique car. His 350 1969 Chevrolet Camaro SS had supposedly sat on the floor at the Chicago Auto Show in 1968. Unfortunately the owner couldn't drive it anymore and put it away. Its redline snow tires are still on the back!

Sometimes owners say they will restore the car "someday." Restoration is rare, but it does happen. Owners can do the work themselves, or they can visit plenty of shops that do classic-car restoration.

The road to restoration isn't always an easy one. The owner's world has changed, and the automotive world changed, too. Things are not as inexpensive as they once were. If you don't want to ruin a camshaft, your older car will need special oil. Mice love to eat up wiring, and fixing that is never cheap. If the vehicle needs serious rust repair, owners discover that bodywork is scarily expensive.

Showing the craziest setup so far, this Chevelle was a total pro-street build. Big engine, big horsepower, big rear tires—the owner had the car running and was just finishing up some odds and ends when he lost interest in his project. It's sat in this old department store for over a decade.

I know a guy who has a bunch of great cars stored in the back of an old warehouse. This nearly all-original 1967 Camaro RS convertible is up there on the cool factor, with black paint, black top, and blue interior.

You rarely see Corvettes in a state of suspended animation. This mid-'70s Vette has been sitting here for a long time. The owner has a few other toys and enjoys them more frequently, and so the Vette sits in the corner, gathering dust.

If you imagine Camaros rotting away as much as I do, you often envision a Disco Era model sitting in a field. Not this one—this is an original 1969 Z/28 Camaro. It doesn't have its original DZ302, but a big-block from a truck. It has been sitting in the yard for a while next to a Disco-era Camaro Z/28. That's more like it.

Most people associate the 1964 Pontiac GTO as the birth of the proper muscle car. I found this 1968 GTO while driving through Wisconsin. It was sitting in the owner's backyard next to the kids' jungle gyms.

The last of the original line of GTO, this 1975 GTO was definitely a looker back in the day, with a shaker hood, red paint, and black vinyl top. Unfortunately time has not been kind to it, and it sat at the side of the road waiting for someone to save it.

Then they get discouraged and the car gets put back in the garage, where it may simply rot.

More time passes and the car never moves from its spot. The day finally comes when owners know they can't fix the car, and they sell it, or they sell because they need the money, or they pass away.

The cars that remain are special. So many others were driven into ditches, taken to the crusher, and turned into coffee cans. The dusty survivors represent small parts of industrial and personal history. I always hope the owner will get back to the car, or maybe the car will go to a family member or even a stranger that happened to show up at just the right time. Then the memory can be shiny and whole again, and allow us a glimpse into a world long past.

Drag racers wanted the lightest, strongest cars to burn down the track the fastest. This 1965 Plymouth Satellite is a post car without a roll-down rear window and extra roof support. Unfortunately this one was tucked into the back of a big barn, and the only thing it is racing is time.

This 1969 Plymouth Fury cop car is rather unique. It's not quite off-the-force fresh, but still has the vintage light bar, among other things. This one has been sitting for a few years at the back of the barn with the '65 Satellite. They definitely haven't seen the sun in a long time.

For a fast pickup truck, you need to consider the 1978 and 1979 Dodge Li'l Red Express. Definitely off the wall, this one was driven into the yard who knows how many decades before. The owner will not sell, and so it sits among other cars, just rusting away.

WIDE-EYED
IN COON VALLEY

When car friends tell you that you need to come see their barn, assume that the trip is going to be worthwhile. Don't let years go by. Sooner is better than later.

Roy and Jamie run MegaParts in Coon Valley, Wisconsin, in the center of Mississippi Valley country. They travel to Mopar shows all over the nation, and whenever I see them, they urge me to come see the cool stuff they have stashed away. They rattle off information about a half-dozen rare 1969 ½ Road Runners and Super Bees. They talk about some Hemi stuff, too. It sounds good—but is it too good to be true? I wondered about that, and I wondered if I really wanted to drive for hours to see for myself.

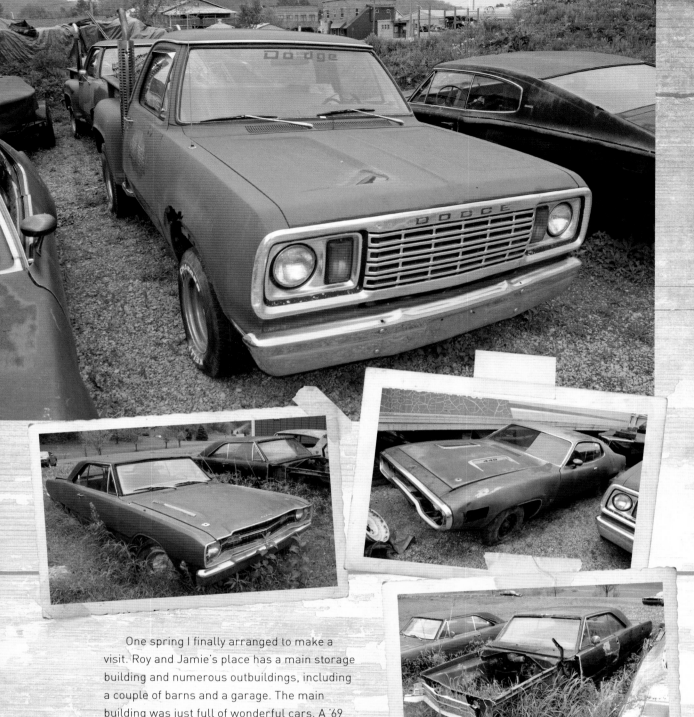

One spring I finally arranged to make a visit. Roy and Jamie's place has a main storage building and numerous outbuildings, including a couple of barns and a garage. The main building was just full of wonderful cars. A '69 Dodge Charger 500 sat near the entrance. For homologation purposes, Dodge built a mere 392 of these, with grille and backlight enhancements designed to reduce drag during NASCAR competition. You don't often see one.

Across from the 500 was a '71 Road Runner, and near that were a few Super Bees and '69 ½ Road Runners. It was an amazing sight.

OK, that was just the first building. After the roof of one of the barns collapsed, Roy and Jamie moved the inventory around back. This part of the stash included multiple Li'l Red Express Trucks and Road Runners, and even the remains of a '66 Hemi Charger.

They led me some distance from the main cluster of buildings to another barn where some of the best cars were stored. Hugging one wall

were multiple '69 ½ Road Runners (I think Roy and Jamie have a thing for them). Way in the back was a 1971 Dodge Super Bee that originated at Mr. Norm's high-performance dealership in Chicago. And next to that was a pair of cars with the 426 Hemi.

With that, I thought we were all done, but my hosts had one more place I had to see. They rent out a house on their property, and behind the house is a garage. Two more vehicles were

inside, but not just any vehicles. I stared at yet another Road Runner, a '69 with the Hemi; and another Li'l Red Express. At a glance, both appeared perfect. Jamie said that the Express would run with a little work, and the only reason the Road Runner hadn't moved in years was a minor ignition issue!

We said our goodbyes and I returned to my hotel. I had seen a lot in a short time, and I just sat there in my room, trying to process it all.

THE TIGHTLY PACKED CORONET R/T

I've been fortunate because my love of vintage cars has allowed me to make friends all over the country. One of them is Dwight. He lives in Wisconsin and knows about stuff I had no idea existed. He told me about a friend who kept cool stuff tucked away in a barn—Dwight just couldn't remember exactly what. We decided to mount a barn-find expedition.

As we pulled up to the property, we noted that there was nothing sitting outside—no old cars, no vintage gas pumps, nothing. The owner came out to greet us, and indicated that we should follow him.

The barn sat at the back of a big, grassy field. An old Dodge pickup was just inside the door. I walked around it and saw the real gold: a two-tone '59 Dodge truck, a 1969 Dodge Coronet R/T, and a 1970 Plymouth Duster.

Dodge based the '69 Coronet R/T on Charger underpinnings, but slotted it as a slightly uplevel ride (the distinction was similar to the one separating the Road Runner from the GTX). This Coronet was presently without an engine, but when new it had a 440 V-8, with a floor-shift 4-speed trans running through a Dana HD rear axle.

The Duster was very basic car originally powered by the indestructible 225-cid slant six. As for the two-tone truck, it was solid, and still had the original poly block 318.

We climbed all over the cars—and I mean actually climbed, because the barn was tightly packed. Every car needed some serious bodywork. The Coronet's missing 440 was an issue, of course, and the Duster was in the middle of an engine swap to a V-8.

Dwight and I didn't buy anything, but you never know about the future. We could always go back!

START
THE DAYTONA

Some of my friendships began on Internet car forums. I met my friend Scott that way, and when he told me he had found something I wouldn't believe, I assembled my expedition gear and headed south. Scott drove his 1970 Plymouth Superbird. I was in my '09 Challenger. No one was going to miss us as we went down the road.

When we got to the owner's house, we saw that he had pushed his prize from the one-car garage where the car had sat for decades. It was a two-owner '69 Dodge Charger Daytona, with just a squish under 125,000 miles on the odometer. The owner said the car had come from a local dealership. He admitted that the Daytona was a real handful to drive—no surprise given the 440 V-8 mated to a 4-speed manual.

In an unexpected moment, the owner

admitted that he used to set beer cans on the Daytona's wing and shoot 'em off with a BB gun! Sure enough, small dents peppered the metal above the rear window.

The fellow washed the car before we arrived, and had hooked a charger to the antique battery. Now we were a bit confused. With nothing more than a "Watch out," the owner did a real no-no—he dumped a pint of gas into the carburetor! We looked on in shock. I asked the owner's wife

if she had a fire extinguisher. She said, "Why?" I realized that I had never seen a Daytona burn to the ground so I just said, "Uh, never mind."

After the motor cranked a bit, it started! None of us could believe it. And it even ran reasonably well.

Because the radiator had very little coolant, the owner shut down the motor after a short while. The three of us pushed the car back into the garage. We thanked the owner and said we'd stay in touch.

And we have—and the Daytona is still in that tiny garage.

PLYMOUTH
HEAVEN

Driving west out of Chicago, I had passed this St. Charles storage lot many times. Something always caught my eye. This time it looked like a muscle car. When I finally had the time to check it out, it blew away all my expectations.

Luck was with me. The lot was a family business, and the car's owner worked there. He was more than happy to show me what was stashed out back.

The first prize I saw was a '68 Plymouth GTX—a nice car by any standard, but particularly desirable because this one came off the line with a 426 Hemi. The owner purchased it, sans engine and transmission, years ago, and left it in his father's lot for safekeeping.

Near the GTX I found a 1970 Charger R/T—a Super Track Pack car with a 440 and a 4-speed.

It was a little rough looking, as though it had been in *Hot Rod*'s Fastest Street Car Shootout at some time in its life.

Way back along the fence line were another

couple of Plymouths. I couldn't quite make them out from a distance, so I was pleased to discover extremely rare 1970 Road Runners that came with the big 440 six barrel! To find one is extraordinary, but two at once is unheard of.

The last car the owner showed us was not as desirable as some of the others, but rare, nonetheless: A 1970 Plymouth Satellite with a 383 big block. This was a slightly detuned version of the standard Road Runner motor. Buyers who wanted the biggest engines sometimes purchased them in basic cars to avoid high insurance premiums that bedeviled most muscle car owners.

This storage lot sat very close to a major city. Rarities aren't found just in the country. If you live in the city, something good may be just a few minutes away.

CHAPTER 3:
ODD CIRCUMSTANCES

Every car collector is interesting, but some are doubly so because they acted when presented with unique, even odd ways to protect their collections. Sometimes an unusual opportunity to store or display a collection just drops into a collector's lap. Other times, the collector actively searches for a unique storage circumstance—and finds one! These "activist" collectors understand the importance of their cars and how to show off and secure their treasures. These people often end up with some of the craziest and most unique adventures anyone can have.

A friend led me onto this weird set—a 1957 Chevrolet 210 and 1958 Impala situated between two Quonset huts in Chicago. One Quonset hut was for media blasting, and the dust completely covered the vehicles inside and out!

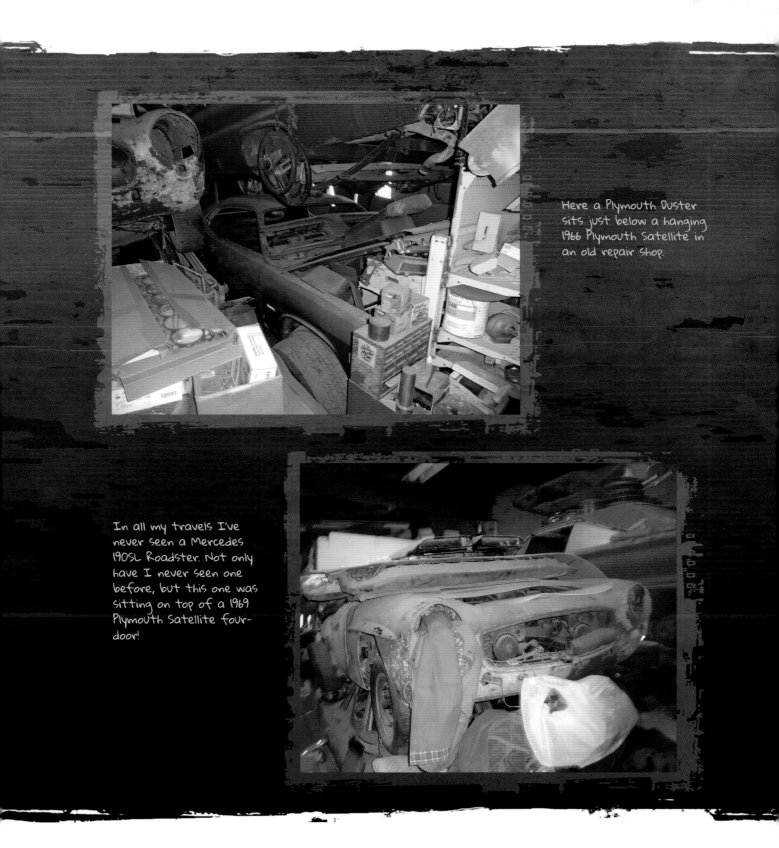

Here a Plymouth Duster sits just below a hanging 1966 Plymouth Satellite in an old repair shop.

In all my travels I've never seen a Mercedes 190SL Roadster. Not only have I never seen one before, but this one was sitting on top of a 1969 Plymouth Satellite four-door!

Hanging from the ceiling next to the 190SL was a 1966 Plymouth Satellite. It had been stripped of paint, hung from the rafters to dry, and left there.

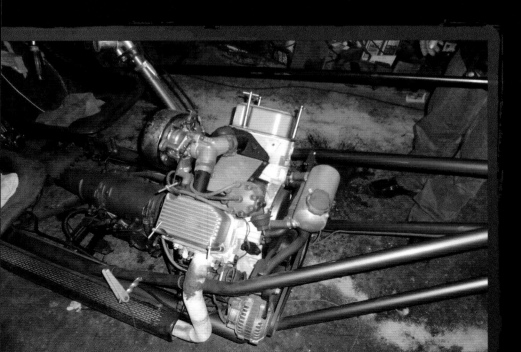

The owner of the 190SL and hanging Satellite also made this incredible trike. He took a Chrysler 400 big-block, cut the front two cylinders off, then made adapter plates and bearing retainers. It's fully functional!

While on a car-search trip I ran into a clean-cut gentleman. I spoke to him for over an hour. He told me that the local school in the small town nearby was going to be auctioned off. After the auction, the old school was likely to be torn down. Well, the gentleman couldn't let that happen. The school was one of those small, turn-of-the-century structures with beautiful architecture; its only problem was that it was run down. So the man bought the school at auction, emptied the place, fixed what was needed, and put his car collection in the old gymnasium! From the outside, you would never know that behind those walls were rows of GM vehicles from the early 1960s!

After getting lost, I came upon a stash of incredible Mopar Muscle cars. One of them ended up being in an old oil tank or something similar. The owner built it into the base of his garage and welded on the doors to keep everything nice and dry!

On the other side of a farm, there were two early-50s Dodge and Plymouth cars just sitting tight in an old tractor shed.

Nineteen-sixty-nine Chevrolet Camaros tend to pop up almost everywhere. People love them. This one was stuck on the second floor of an old General Store.

Cows munching on hay is usually what you find in the cow pasture—not a 1969 Dodge Super Bee! I was told it had crashed into a cement wall, then parted out and put into the cow field to be used as a rubbing post.

Collectors of this sort think outside the box when it comes to protecting their cars. They own the equivalent of fine china, but they're not going to keep it in a drawer or attic. They want a china cabinet. So they make things happen. They buy the abandoned schools or churches. They even do the completely unexpected.

I was traveling through Wisconsin, looking for a old Dodge Travco my friend had said was for sale. Instead, I ended up semi-lost in a small town. I slowly drove down the road and came across a family that owned a large quantity of preserved Mopars. These folks had devised all sorts of incredible ways to protect the cars they loved. They hit on a particularly ingenious method as they looked at the freshly dug foundation of their new garage. Their property was littered with old oil

This Chevrolet Nova sits in an old freight elevator in a small town. It hasn't moved in years, and the elevator hasn't moved longer than that.

Friends are always a good source for crazy cars. One of mine told me about a bunch of great vehicles sitting in the middle of a cornfield. He wasn't kidding—look at this early-'70s Oldsmobile 442!

This is one of the oddest cars I had ever come across. It's a 1968 Dodge Dart 4-door that's been cut down into a "compact" 2-door! Never seen anything like it.

tanks, and the family incorporated some right into the foundation. That way, especially valuable cars could be rolled right under the garage and, when needed, rolled right out again. And if you've ever wondered what happens to old vinyl billboard signs, well, this family used them in the yard, as car covers! Whatever works, right?

With the recent dip in real estate values, the purchase of property becomes a more viable option for many. Factories, warehouses, and other large structures are coming on the market at low prices. Sometimes these bargains show up in the big cities, but you'll find most of them in smaller cities and towns, often in places that have seen better days. People pick up entire blocks of buildings for pennies on the dollar and use them to store anything and everything.

Backed up to the field was the rarest car of the bunch—a 1968 Pontiac GTO Convertible, a 400-ci V-8 with a 4-on-the-floor. Once the star of the muscle car era, now it lacks an engine and transmission, though the owner intends to restore it soon. I sure hope so.

Right off the road, you can't help but notice this 1969 Chrysler Newport sitting on the back of a vintage car hauler. The craziest part was the owner put a rare long ram induction setup from an earlier Chrysler on there!

I have a friend who taught me about hot rods. He also had some extremely rare French Fords–a pair of Ford Comète Monte Carlos powered by flathead V-8s with 4-speeds. Only made for a handful of years, few made it to the US.

Here in Chicago, I went to the wedding of friends. The ceremony was held inside a rehabbed old factory where the painting of billboards and other signage had been done. A room on the third floor had incredible windows where artwork could be viewed in natural light. That was impressive, but the ballroom was amazing because the walls were lined with classic cars. The owner had turned the dilapidated factory into the home for his collection! The immaculate cars were framed with vintage automotive neon; the whole room was a real showplace. And from the street, no one would guess that any of this existed. From the outside, the building still looked like an old factory.

Here's the second of the Ford Comète Monte Carlos; they had both been buried for decades.

Firebirds are not common—you're more likely to find Camaros. The owner of this 1969 Pontiac Firebird is in the process of being turned into a Trans Am tribute—a fine project.

Tucked next to the 1969 Firebird was another long-term project—a real 1965 Pontiac GTO. The owner cut out all the rust and was in the process of installing the correct patch panels for it.

People can go to extreme lengths to protect their cars. In small towns, collectors tuck cars away in barns, corncribs, and even old stores. In the cities, you'll find them stashed in old factories and warehouses. All of this means that many cars remain hidden and out of sight for years and even decades. The options are as endless as the human imagination. If someone wants to protect something, the person will do whatever is necessary.

Sitting behind a body shop in a small fenced-in area was a trio of rare cars. Vines had overtaken them all, and this 1968 GTO convertible got the worst of it—the vines took advantage of the topless wonder to spread their tendrils a bit.

Hiding on the far side was a 1968 Pontiac Firebird. It's just a bare shell, but for sitting in Wisconsin it's still a decent builder.

Between the two Pontiacs was the only Chevrolet in the group. It was nothing to sneeze at—an original 1964 Impala SS.

This rare late-'50s Lincoln 2-door sits forlorn in a yard where the treeline slowly moves past. Soon you won't be able to get it out at all!

For sitting in a northern state, this 1957 Cadillac and 1957 Oldsmobile are still in good shape. They have a great patina for sitting outside all these years.

You would never have known there was a junkyard deep in the forest. The trees have enveloped everything, including this 1974 Dodge Dart Sport 340.

As I helped a friend clean out a closed auto parts store that had opened in the 1930s, we came across items squirreled away in all corners of the property—which was nearly a city-block long. There were carbs for Model As in the rafters, head gaskets for a Jeep in the bathroom. Out back was an early '50s Dodge that was cut in half, crossways. The craziest thing we found, though, was behind a small door that led to a room holding an old VW and a 1972 Chevrolet Monte Carlo! The owner had built the room around these cars, and not with 2 x 4s, either, but entirely in brick. What prompted that person to go to so much trouble and expense? Nobody knows.

It always comes back to the why—why do people put forth such effort? Is it because they know they have a rare car and want to protect it? Do they have a sentimental attachment? Sometimes

Rows of rare muscle cars and vintage cars are hidden in the forest. This 1970 Plymouth Barracuda sits next to its predecessor, a 1968 Barracuda, in nearly identical blues.

The three Barracudas—a pair of 1968s and a 1970—sit in the forest that has consumed them.

Originally a Lime-Light Green 1970 Barracuda, this model has been sitting so long it's been completely consumed by the forest.

A few more rare cars slowly being reclaimed by the earth include a 1970 Plymouth Barracuda and a 1977 Plymouth Road Runner. By 1977, the Road Runner was based on the F-body Volare.

Sitting through the years and overtaken by the forest, this poor 1968 Plymouth Barracuda convertible has had its entire top just destroyed over time, rusting out nearly the entire floor.

the reason is one or the other, but usually it's both. Even the smallest attachment is enough to encourage people to tuck away their cars "for a rainy day." They may hope to return to the cars when the time is right, and restore them to past glory. Some tucked-away gems are revisited and restored. You see them at car shows and on the road. For others, the toll of time is just too much, and they decay until they are beyond help.

Fortunately, the decay is slowed when the imaginations of ingenious collectors are fired by the unexpected.

Just about the only Ford product in the forest, this 1970 Ford Mustang in Grabber Blue has a vinyl top treatment that nobody seems to have seen before.

You just never know what you might come across. Deep in Wisconsin, my friends and I encountered one of the first, if not the first, Musgrave Racing Enterprises car hauling trucks, with custom sleeping area and car bed.

IOWA
RAIL

As I prepared to travel to a certain part of Iowa, I asked users of a Mopar Internet forum if they knew of any cool cars sitting around out there. My reputation as a good keeper of secrets helped out, and people gladly shared information about hidden goodies.

One of the leads seemed especially promising, and I was pleased to get the owner on the phone. He told me to come on out and see what he had. So on a Friday afternoon I drove to the middle of Iowa.

The gentleman owned a junkyard. Nothing unusual about that—other than that most of the yard sat on an abandoned railroad right of way. That was unique.

The owner gave me free rein to walk around and photograph whatever I wished. He had a variety of nifty cars dating from the 1940s to the present day. I walked down one row to discover a '58 Dodge Coronet, and a '70 Challenger down another. I turned a corner and found a '67

Firebird, and something from around the turn of the twenty-first century. The selection was a real mix, and I really didn't know what might pop up next. That was when the real surprise revealed itself.

The middle of the property had been an old railroad depot. The building was there, and so were all the old signals and railroad boxes. There seemed to be a little bit of everything. When the owner bought the property after the rail line closed, he bought all these rail artifacts, too, and now they just lay around in piles.

I walked the rest of the yard and saw a lot of incredible pieces. I thanked the owner, who invited me to come back anytime!

PSYCHO
BEES

The Mopar Car Club has counted me as a member for many years. At least once a year a group of us will jump in my car and just drive around northern Illinois, looking for old cars. Our very first trip was hard to beat.

Legends about some particular cars had circulated for years. I had heard the stories for as long as I'd been a car guy. But no outsiders had ever seen them up close or gotten pictures of them. This amounted to a sort of challenge, so my friends and I decided to see if this celebrated stash could be located. Well, we got one heck of a surprise.

One spot out in the country looked promising. From the road we saw a farmhouse—and a '66 Chevy Chevelle SS 396 and a '69 Dodge Charger R/T. Parked with aft ends facing the street were a 1970 Dodge Super Bee and a '68 Dodge Coronet 500.

Wow.

We parked and knocked on the door. The family was friendly, and let us check out the cars and see what was what. We stepped around the outside of the house and were blown away. From

the street, we hadn't been able to see a pair of Challengers—a rare Rallye model and a basic small-block V-8. Both were in really good shape.

We left the Challengers and found the car that really took the cake: a 1970 Super Bee painted all over in tiny, psychotic bees! Some of the bees were eating road runners. Other road runners had bees popping out of their heads. The car's trunk lid said, "Straight from the Hive." This was the handiwork of

the present owner, and it was great.

The '69 Charger had been altered as well, with a 1970 Super Bee center scoop that had been molded to the hood. It was definitely unique!

We stayed for quite a while, chatting with the family and learning that the place used to be a dairy farm specializing in cheese. The business was long gone, and now the cars sat on the ruins of the barns. I don't expect to ever hear a story quite like it again.

MISSOURI
LIMESTONE

As you're being driven into the middle of nowhere by a guy you know only from the Internet, you pause to consider that it isn't the best of ideas . . . usually. But car nuts who frequent the Internet often know where the best cars are hiding. I had been on many car-hunting expeditions, but this one was going to be a first.

The junkyard sat on the remains of an old quarry. The story goes that the family bought the property a long time ago, and began placing cars on and around the Missouri limestone. When the quarry was active, diggers cut caves into the hills in order to get at the stone. As the junkyard grew, the owners started to fill the caves with cars!

The yard once had some real rarities, like a barn-kept 1970 Plymouth Superbird that was sold for cash.

The caves that we saw were mostly empty, and the yard was much smaller than during its glory days. Despite that, the place had quite a collection of unique and interesting vehicles. The barn alone had a Torino GT, an Oldsmobile from the 1950s, a '67 Camaro, and even an old dirt tracker made from a Ford.

Most of the cars lived outside. We found a Ford panel van from the '30s, and a '69 Firebird ragtop. Another car with a floor-mounted 4-speed, a '67 Sport Fury convertible, was there. In the weeds out back we found a 1969 AMC AMX.

The yard was an unusual place, and a good reminder that it's smart to check up on every lead and go down every narrow road.

TRACTOR-TRAILER CARS

Sometimes I go against my gut. I want to discover old cars, but I get the feeling that I shouldn't do a particular thing, or go somewhere that seems promising. Sometimes, the evidence just isn't compelling enough.

For years, I had driven past a 1973 Dodge Charger that sat in a storage yard. I always took note of the place but never followed up. The car wasn't one that I was seriously interested in. One day, though, I had some free time, and pulled in.

The owner was outside, working on a truck. I mentioned the Charger. He pointed to the middle distance. "You see all those tractor trailers out there? They're full of old cars!"

We walked through the yard and started opening the trailers. One was full of rare Mopar parts. Another housed an old Buick with an air ride setup. Another had a 1970 Dodge Challenger R/T, and farther down was a '70 Road Runner. And this was just the first batch!

Another row of trailers sat across the main yard. Each of them had a car inside, sometimes two. One held a '72 Charger and a '67 Ford

Falcon. A '71 Super Bee and a '71 Plymouth GTX were in another. The trailers and cars just kept coming.

The last cars the owner wanted me to see were not in trailers, but despite the lack of protection, they were some of the rarest on the place. I guess you'd call them foolers, because at a glance they didn't suggest desirability. Both were '69 Dodge Dart GTSs. They were M-Code

440s, two of only about 640 homologation specials made for the model year. Dodge came up with the package as an answer to the NASCAR success of big-block Chevy Novas and Ford Mustangs. Now these Darts were shells of race cars, the original wrap-over stripes that started on the rear quarter panels barely visible.

This time I had listened to my gut and found something wonderful.

CHAPTER 4:
TOO FAST TO LIVE, TOO YOUNG TO DIE

The allure of performance cars can take over a person's life. Many people are susceptible to this, but particularly the ones who toil in the garage until the late hours of the night, or well into morning, to make a carburetor work right, or resolve a brake problem. These guys are car guys. Many of them grew up with muscle cars in their lives. Back then, muscle meant high horsepower in small and mid-size bodies. The mindset can be traced back to hot rods of the 1940s and '50s. It was all about speed or looks then, and sometimes a bit of both. The production muscle car began to take hold in the early 1960s. Some guys with the rarest of the rare got hold of them when the cars were new or nearly new, or later, when they were just used cars and gas guzzlers. The smartest and most dedicated of those gearheads knew what they had and put their cars away for a rainy day.

This is a car of myth and legend, one that people tell stories of for years to come. An original 1969 Dodge Charger Daytona sits outside, neglected for decades. For shame!

You could see this car from the road, and I finally got the nerve to ask the owner to see the car up close. It turned out to be a 1969 Dodge Coronet 500, a model between the 440 and R/T.

An old barn in Illinois housed a bunch of cool cars and trucks. This is an original 1979 Dodge Li'l Red Express truck, tucked up against the wall with its original exhaust stacks intact.

Getting lost sometimes ends up being for the best, as I found a nice family in Wisconsin by accident with a barn full of Mopars, including this 1969 Dodge Super Bee.

The same family as above had another 1970 Dodge Super Bee in a lean-to next to the barn. This is a rare V-Code 440 Six-Barrel, sitting in front of a 1969 Dodge Coronet R/T.

I'm a member of a local car club called the Chicago Gearheads. We are a medium-sized club, and a good group of guys. Earlier in the book you read about one of our members, who invited me to view a car he bought new (with some help from his mother). Even as a kid, he was a true gearhead. He knew that the car he was buying was unique and rare, and he protected that car through his entire life. He made sure that it was taken care of. That's why the car came to sit for decades in a Chicagoland garage—a unique, hard-to-find race car that never changed hands. The owner had the forethought to keep it all these years; it's the kind of decision that pays off in the end. This owner enjoys the memories associated with the car and has seen monetary gain, as well, as the car's value has skyrocketed due to the rarity of the model/engine combination.

Not to be left out, they had a few Challengers lying around as well. This 1972 Dodge Challenger resides in the basement of one of the barns.

At car shows, you'll see many vintage muscle cars produced by GM, Ford, and Mopar. They are available today not because they were produced in plentiful numbers, but because their runs were relatively limited. Some were driven to death; others just faded into the dust of old age. Surviving examples are rare, and rarity increases desirability. And car guys knew what was rare. When they heard "Hemi" or "Shelby" or "Yenko," they knew the car was special, and deserved special care. More of those cars were preserved than, say, slant six Dusters or 4-door Impalas. The trickle-down effect has been that a greater proportion of muscle cars survived. Devoted owners saw to it that these cars are around to be enjoyed today.

One of their storage barns held nothing but B-Body Mopars, a '69 Satellite, '69 Charger, and a '70 Charger, among others.

It is good to have friends who like to travel. My friend Mark pointed out this 1970 Dodge Challenger in Plum Crazy paint sitting in a yard in Wisconsin.

After all these years, I am not surprised by much. I had actually been to this junkyard before, but the owner let me into a barn for the first time, where he stored a C1 Chevrolet Corvette! Color me surprised.

After the Hot Rod Power Tour one year, I headed to Charlotte, North Carolina to visit my sister. En route, I discovered this little honey hole in the mountains. Out front was an all-original 1955 Chevrolet 2-door post—one of the famous Tri-Fives.

Talking with the owner, he said if I was interested in muscle cars, I should walk around back, where a 1969 Chevrolet Chevelle sat next to a 1969 Dodge Charger.

That's very like the situation of my friend with the Hemi Charger 500, who is discussed in this chapter. While out on the road, he loved to find—and buy— rare cars. Because he had a thing for Mopars, many would be located and brought back to his farm. He even collected the rarest of the rare Mopar parts. Most such parts disappeared into history, so here he is decades later, with an amazing collection. Because of his dedication, the parts survived to exist in the modern era.

Sitting in Charlotte, North Carolina was a Mopar car dealer. You would never know unless you slowed down off the highway, but in his back lot he had a smorgasbord of cool cars, including this 1969 Plymouth GTX.

The Charger was right up against a ridge that fell drastically into a mountain river. Any more decent rain and the Charger would be in the drink!

You don't see this very often, but as North Carolina is the home of Richard Petty, I found this 1972 Plymouth Barracuda in Petty Blue.

This is what happens when you don't pay your bills—they take half your car! This 1970 Plymouth Road Runner was parted out to save other cool cars.

Tucked in the back of the yard, this complete 1968 Plymouth Road Runner was slowly being re-absorbed by the Earth.

As noted, many muscle cars of the classic era were collected after the fact, in the late 1970s and early '80s. Back then, the gas crunch doomed muscle cars to gas-guzzling dinosaur status. Popular wisdom was that such cars should be relegated to junkyards. Many of them were. Even fresh off the production line, they didn't have the best rust proofing or fit and finish. Rust was a major bugaboo. Grocery getters and muscle cars alike were beat up pretty good as they got passed down the family tree. Most ended as rusty hulks in junkyards. But muscle aficionados took care of their rides, particularly if they drove a GTO Judge, an AAR 'Cuda, COPO Camaro, or other obvious rarity. Many of

Next to the '68 Road Runner was a '69 model—this one had been there so long that a grove of trees had grown up through the engine compartment.

Nothing like cruising in a convertible to make a person enjoy life. This 1969 Plymouth Barracuda convertible had not done that in many years.

A 1973 Dodge Challenger sits wide open in the back lot, waiting for its time in the shop.

American Motors Corporation really pushed the envelope with the AMX 2-door. This 1969 AMC AMX had seen better days, but was a great project car.

A friend of mine got his 1969 Camaro Z/28 that way. He bought it back in the '80s, when the cars were plentiful and cheap. He found a very nice, clean Camaro and began to play around with it. Someone who had the car before him had done some poor engine work. A valve dropped, damaging the piston and block. So what does a person in that situation do? My buddy pulled the bad engine, found a junkyard engine, and threw it in the car. But because he knew the Z/28 was something special, he kept the original, damaged engine tucked away in his garage. He also made a point to keep as many of the original parts as he could. Now, decades later, he's thankful he did, because all those original parts add hugely to the Camaro's value.

Rare as hell, this is a 1954 Kaiser Manhattan. What made it special was its original McCulloch Supercharger.

Out back behind a body shop was this original steel body Ford Model A 2-door sedan. The owner plans to eventually make it into a hot rod.

Another rare vehicle sitting behind the shop was an old Cab Over Engine truck (COE) that was being transformed into a hot-rodded car carrier.

ong the bushes was this 1969 Plymouth Barracuda. The stripe could mean it was a high-
formance model. Unfortunately little remained to say exactly what it was.

Car enthusiasts are everywhere. The come from America's fields and farms, and from the
el canyons of major cities. There is little difference between them in spirit, but not everyone has
ual ability to a car. In the cities, space is at a premium. You can't store a car, even a rare one, over
long term without paying through the nose. That's why so many desirable cars are located far
m the city, in the suburbs and farmlands. Collectors from those areas have much more space at
ir disposal, and can preserve their treasures more easily, and more privately .

s is what remained of a 1950 Plymouth Business Coupe. The owner wanted to build a clone
the original RameLamarno '49 Plymouth race car, called The High and Mighty.

Walking among the scrubs, you don't expect to come across an original 1971 Plymouth Duster 340 with the original 340 sticker still visible on the deteriorating hood.

The 1971 Dodge Demon had a few different models if you wanted all the looks of the 340 without the engine, like this original 318 Demon Sizzler with original graphics intact.

The trees have enveloped this poor 1972 Dodge Demon in rare Petty Blue. It has sat for so long that the trees have completely encircled the car.

Up in Wisconsin, I had a friend who had a large storage barn. He kept it full of tractors and hay for his cows. Years earlier, though, the barn had been home to horses and other animals. But farming had changed, and with the animals gone, a bunch of empty stalls were available to be filled. So what did he do? He bought cars. He had some rare ones too, including old race cars and a '69 Charger R/T. There were others, too. Because he had the room, my friend was able to protect his cars much more easily and at a lower cost than people in the city.

The dedicated car collectors have great love for their machines, but they have insight, too. Call it a sense of history, call it respect for the past—it's a quality that allows collectors to see beyond the moment. They see the future as well as the past. Their imagination is why I and so many other car lovers are continually surprised and delighted.

Trees take no prisoners, but time does some funny things to the land. Not only have trees grown up, through and around this 1970 Plymouth Barracuda, but the hill it was pointed toward has eroded and now partially covers the front of the car.

Most people would not believe you if you told them that deep in the forest is a 1968 Dodge Charger R/T. And yet, there it was, sitting so long a tree had grown up and around the front bumper.

Now there is rare, and then there is the uber rar,. the cars that people don't know exist, and shouldn't. This is a 1972 Plymouth Road Runner 440 Six Barrel—one of one. This was the only known build before the engine option was dropped. In the right hands, it's priceless, and even features a sun roof.

CHALLENGERS
AND THE HEMI

Have you ever heard stories about places that don't make sense? I mean, places that just shouldn't exist. A wall of shaker hoods from rare Mopars? What sense does that make? Rows of Challengers tucked away inside while a Superbird sits outside? Odd. I had heard stories about such a place for years, and never put much store in them until someone offered to introduce me to the owner. That was the day that reality changed for me.

The owner was very cordial to my friend and me. As a little kitten skipped around at our feet, he walked us to a barn. First thing I noticed inside was the '70 Superbird nose sitting on a workbench. We went in deeper and there it was: the mythical wall of shaker hoods. I couldn't believe it.

The cars were nothing to sneeze at, either. I saw an altered-wheelbase '65 Hemi Satellite and a 1970 Challenger 440 Six Pack convertible.

There was a '71 Barracuda convertible and a '70 Hemi Challenger. All of this in one small barn!

It didn't end there. Another barn had more cars. The structure was classic barn red, and sticking from the entrance was a 1970 Challenger R/T. That was a rarity—and even more Challenger R/Ts were inside, plus a '70 Charger R/T.

Another quite different kind of rarity was behind the barn, an original 1970 Dodge Dude

Sweptline pickup, pitched when it was new by Barney Fife himself, Don Knotts. During the truck's 1970-71 run, Dodge built fewer than 2,000.

We went deeper onto the property. More Challengers were scattered about, including a '71 ragtop with a tree growing up through the body. We saw Darts, Dusters, and Barracudas. There was a bit of it all there.

We were getting ready to leave when the owner pointed to a car under a blue tarp. It was a '70 Plymouth Superbird! Out front, sitting quietly in the driveway was a 1964 Dodge Polara convertible. Nothing too crazy about that, until we popped the hood and saw the original 426 Hemi. I nearly fell over.

Great things can be hidden inside unassuming packages. It was a good lesson.

BIRDS IN
THE BARN

My first "barn find" came about completely by accident. I was at an auction—waiting for a '53 New Yorker shell with a 354 Hemi to go across the block—when a gentleman told me about a fellow living nearby with a yard full of Mopars.

When I didn't win the New Yorker, I booked over to the Mopar yard. My eyes popped wide open because, sure enough, I saw Chargers, Road Runners, and a Super Bee or two. I chatted with the owner, and after awhile he led me to his storage barn. He mentioned that he had a Superbird inside. Now, even with him being a Mopar guy, I figured he meant Super Bee. There was no way he had one of just 1,920 Plymouth winged wonders. (The official Plymouth production figure is 1,920; it is possible that more than that came off the line.)

He tugged at the door and there it was: a real 1970 Plymouth Superbird resting quietly on the dirt floor. I couldn't believe it. You just never heard about such a rare and unique car just sitting around. And yet, there it was, right in front of me.

That was the beginning of my long friendship with the owner. I come back every few years to talk and have another look at his collection. And during every visit, I discover something I'd missed before—like the rusting hulk I spotted squatting on a trailer. It was a Ramo Stott 1971 Hemi Road Runner, retired from NASCAR competition and turned into a dirt-track racer.

It thrills me to have a close look at that kind of history.

HEAVY STUFF
IN IOWA

After years of hearing stories about a place of dreams and wonders, I was finally able to get out to an Iowa farm where the tales—people said—came true.

I met the owner, who was excited to show me his goodies. I offered him the issue of *Hot Rod* with my article about an original-owner '69 Dodge Charger Daytona. He looked at the magazine and said he had one of those cars that the Daytona was made from. It was an odd way to put it, and I assumed he meant a '69 Charger.

Our first stop was his tractor shed. He kept a '69 Charger 500 in there, an original 426 Hemi example that came with a floor-mounted 4-speed and a body done up in Dodge's B5 Blue. The sad thing is that the car had sunk into the earth right up to the rims' valve stem caps.

Other cars were in the shed: a 1967 Plymouth Hemi GTX, a '67 GTX with the 440, and a smattering of Plymouths and Dodges spanning the 1940s to the '60s.

Out in the "back 40" the owner kept rows of rare Mopars, including a '64 Plymouth Fury; an original Max Wedge car sitting with other Dodge Coronets; Plymouth Barracudas. There were more, a lot more—rows of cars that covered the property from one end to the other.

I had already been flabbergasted by this visit, but things just got better. The guy kept trailers for storage; some were full of rare dual carb setups; others were stuffed with first-generation Hemi engines, including an original Hemi irrigation pump in its original stand! Now I understood the owner's remark about Charger Daytonas.

The interior of the last barn was dim, but I saw at least three 426 Hemis, and benches covered in spare Hemi parts. You couldn't walk without tripping over something 426 Hemi. And here's the craziest: a complete, original NASCAR Hemi setup. You just don't see that!

The owner was a truck driver. He loved rare stuff and found a lot of it during his travels. He favored Mopar, so those cars and parts dominated his collection.

The gentleman has one of the greatest collections I've ever seen.

SLEEPING
AERO WARRIORS

Sometimes I really have to beat the ground to locate a certain car or collection. Other times, the treasures fall into my lap. Thanks to the Internet, this adventure was one of the "lap" stories.

I left a Monday-afternoon phone message for the owner of a property, asking if I might come down and photograph his collection. He called back and turned out to be an amiable guy. We set up a time for my visit, but he warned that the Internet glimpse of his collection represented just a small fraction of what he had.

The drive ate up half a day, which I didn't mind at all as soon as the owner began to show me around the property. First thing we looked at wasn't a car but a vintage Indian motorcycle that belonged to my host's father. Close by, a converted mobile home protected a 1969 Dodge Charger Daytona; an improbably low-mileage, NASCAR-inspired Dodge Aspen Kit Car—and a 1970 Hemi 'Cuda!

It was when we moved into the main barn that things went sideways. The building was crammed with rare collectibles. As if an omen of things to come, a '66 Hemi Charger was closest to the entrance. We walked a little farther, and there on the right was a mid-'70s Cosworth Vega. A '69 Charger 500 was next, and then a 1969 Ford Talladega.

Then there was the other side of the barn, where I found a big-block '69 Plymouth Sport Satellite convertible with a 4-speed; whoever ordered it that way knew how to dodge the insurance man.

I was impressed by a '69 Mercury Cyclone Spoiler II, and then I was floored by a 1970 Plymouth Superbird!

The owner came down with the Mopar bug in the mid- to late '70s, and picked up his prizes when they were just used cars. After he bought the '70 'Cuda he phoned his girlfriend and said he had something special to show her. She thought he was talking about an engagement ring. Well . . . surprise! (She was a good sport and ended up marrying him anyway.)

It's easy to admire the Mopar aero warriors, but you won't be taken seriously by the community unless you own one. My host figured there was no reason why he couldn't own one of each! That's what he found, and he's had them ever since.

CHAPTER 5:
THE PATIENT CANNOT BE SAVED

There are times when people care too much about a car. They have the best of intentions to "restore it someday." But without proper protection over the years, the car just rots away. Many of these owners aren't truly neglectful; time just gets away from them. They don't want to lose their strong connections to the cars. They may neglect the vehicles, but they still want that connection. But when the car is gone, so is the connection.

Many old race cars get pushed out back and forgotten. This 1971 Dodge Dart in Plum Crazy Purple is no different.

This poor 1964 Plymouth Fury sits neglected next to a grouping of Mopars. It has sat so long that trees, not engines, have taken up residence in the engine compartment.

Something you will never see is a Suzuki LJ20. It was basically Suzuki's knockoff of a Jeep. Few were exported to the US, and even fewer survive today. This one has been sitting a while.

A 1965 Ford Mustang should be roaming the open roads, not sitting in this junkyard. We're going to have to find a name for the old "tree-through-the-hood" maneuver.

Convertibles always get beat up the worst when sitting, and this 1969 Plymouth Road Runner is no exception. The entire back of the car has completely disintegrated.

If that kind of relationship seems a little mixed-up, you may be right. Other times, car owners who enjoy the envious responses of others are nevertheless frozen into that peculiar immobility that encourages decay. Even though the car gives the collector a sense of worth, it's allowed to fall into such disrepair that, finally, the machine is only good for parts—if and when the owner decides to sell.

I've seen this in my travels more times than I can count. "I'm going to restore it someday" is a line that's become very familiar to me. Unfortunately, many of the cars in question are well beyond help: Chevelles with rotted-out frames or Mustangs with front ends missing, rusting away into the ground. The owners may think they're serious about restoration, but don't think about the dollars and cents required to actually put together a car from a rotted hulk. And sometimes, when they do find out, they realize they can't manage it, so a car sits even longer.

Military vehicles are made to take a beating and still keep working. This old military vehicle was driven into the yard, but has sat so long that the owner hasn't been able to get it running in years.

There are some vehicles you don't see sitting much, and this 1958 DeSoto Sportsman with Hemi power still under the hood is definitely one of them, though it's rusted pretty badly.

A vintage car is a physical connection to the past. What an incredible gift. It's the car that you took your wife out on dates with, or drove the day you brought your baby home from the hospital. There is always some sort of connection between the car and meaningful, precious moments. Because of that, many people just can't let their car go. That's how you end up with a pile of rust.

Certainly, the owners have the right to let that happen. It's their property, they can do with it as they please. But the day will come when the car is too far gone to be saved. After that, the car may vanish altogether, and the owner is apt to feel terrible about the loss.

Later in this section, we'll meet a gentleman with plenty of cool cars. He has an Impala SS convertible, a DeSoto with a first-generation Hemi—but the real kicker is three early C1 Corvettes. One had been in a wreck and was parked in an old box truck. Another was just a busted-up hulk. The third was the nicest of the bunch, red and white, and complete from bumper to bumper. However, because the owner had an emotional attachment to the cars, he wasn't going to sell. Instead, he

People think tarps help keep cars protected, but most of the time they just keep moisture trapped and accelerate deterioration. This 1966 Chevrolet Impala SS Convertible had seen better days before the tarp.

Another poor Hemi-powered DeSoto sits derelict in the yard, with the Hemi still there in the ribcage of the car.

Under a collapsed garage roof sat a 1959 Chevrolet El Camino. The owner said it was a nice car when he put it in the garage, but time got away from him and then the garage

When you think of a Corvette, you think of this car. This is a 1956 Chevrolet Corvette. The owner had three of similar vintage around his property, but unfortunately this was the nicest one of the bunch. It's not completely beyond hope, but it will need some serious elbow grease.

let them sit. And while most of a Corvette is fiberglass, the frame surely isn't, and this complete example had been sitting in the mud so long the metal was coming off in chunks. Modern technology allows a car of this type and in this condition to be restored, but the investment is significant.

Vintage cars turn up in all sorts of places, but the ones that are beyond help are usually the ones out in the open. Some get to sit under a blue tarp. You would think that a tarp helps preserve the car from the elements. Unfortunately, the tarp traps moisture between the plastic and the car, causing the car to rust out faster. People don't realize this, and over the years the cars slowly turn to oxide.

Neglect of this sort is less common in the more densely populated cities, where there is far less room to keep a car, and ordinances prevent backyard storage. So you'll usually see these cars out in the country, where they have room to, well, sit. You can't drive down a country road without seeing a

Near that '59 El Camino in the same collapsed garage was this old early-'50s MG roadster. Complete stem to stern, this car had seen better days, and a collapsed garage on top of it didn't help.

Someone loved
this car so much
they painted CUDA
in big letters
on the rear
quarter panels.
Unfortunately
they didn't love it
enough to save it
from its fate in
the junkyard.

few old cars and trucks tucked way back on somebody's property. Why send it to the junkyard when the owner can just leave it on the property? Maybe it can be restored someday.

I've come across many scenes like this in my travels. Earlier in the book I described a 1969 Dodge Super Bee that had been in an accident; somehow, it had been run into a wall. The owner's family had a farm, so instead of scrapping the car and sending it to the junkyard, the Bee was picked clean of reusable parts and then dumped into the grazing field for the cows to use as a rubbing post! And for the past 20 years that's been the situation. The cows have enjoyed it, but now the Super Bee is certainly beyond help. And of the parts that remain, few are usable. But if the Bee had been left in a location where the cows couldn't get to it, it might still be restorable.

Then there is the other side of the coin, divorced from sentiment and even from driving. Back when vintage muscle cars were cheap, people bought loads of them for spare parts. Why not buy a few first-gen Camaros—the parts interchange for the most part. Even just a decade ago, some

Sitting in a pasture, this '20s- or '30s-era car with wood wheels had probably driven its last mile well over half a century ago. Now it just sits in the weeds and wheat in an Illinois junkyard.

This poor first-generation Camaro sits in the wheat, revealing hack-job flairs in the back (probably to fit bigger tires). Somewhere along the line it was given up on and pushed into the yard, never to run again.

muscle cars could still be found cheap. When the premeditated scavenging was done and the parts were plucked, the cars were pushed way back on the property to rust away.

That sort of thing is certainly common enough, and it can be good news for other collectors. For example, I bought a guy's collection of E-body parts and shells of vehicles. He used to be heavily involved in the Mopar hobby, but for decades there was little aftermarket support for Challengers and 'Cudas. His solution was to buy as many as he could in order to keep his one or two cars alive.

The rarest one I got my hands on was a 1971 Plymouth Barracuda convertible. It had no options, just plain manual steering, manual drum brakes, manual top, slant six, 3-speed manual on the

Looking proud, this 1972 Plymouth Sport Satellite sits nose-high all by itself. It's not a bad project but would take an extraordinary amount of work to get it out of the yard.

Cool stripes were the norm in the mid-'70s. This 1974 Dodge Dart Sport in blue at one point had a neat stripe that deteriorated over time, leaving its outline in the patina.

This was at one time the least-optioned 1971 Barracuda convertible. It was as basic as you can get—smallest engine, smallest transmission, manual everything. It was a rare car, but sadly rusted beyond repair.

For a person who knows Mopars, the stripe on this car automatically gets your heart racing. Thinking it was a rare 1970 Plymouth AAR 'Cuda, it turned out to be just a 1970 383 with AAR stripes.

Cruising down the road, this Plum Crazy Purple 1970 Dodge Challenger must have been a real looker instead of the rusted hulk it is now.

floor. But it was a real '71 Barracuda ragtop. It had the same body as the $5 million 1971 Hemi 'Cuda convertibles that roll through the big auctions every year. Yet way back when, this one was nothing but a parts car. So it sat outside, next to a lake, for decades. The car rusted away so badly it was in at least three different pieces.

Sadly, the 1971 Barracuda convertible could not be saved. But other great cars are still out there, waiting to be found and preserved.

Rusting away in someone's yard is sad, but a premature end is even sadder. This 1979 Dodge Li'l Red Express truck ended up getting rolled at a good clip and is now just a parts donor.

Most people don't even know what a Jeep FC is, but they were made for many years. This Jeep FC (Forward Control) looks to have at one point been a boom truck or tow truck.

Being reclaimed by the forest is no way for a 1970 Plymouth Road Runner to die, but here this shell of a car in Plum Crazy Purple sits as it slowly rots into the ground.

In 1971 the Dodge Super Bee moved over onto the Dodge Charger lineup for one year before being dropped. This is a basic 1971 Dodge Charger Super Bee sitting deep in a forest.

I've got a soft spot for Dodge RamChargers as I had an amazing 1993 unit, but like this '78 RamCharger, it rusted away nearly to the point of beyond help. This one, with the original removable top, is well beyond anyone's help.

Surrounded by leaves and trees for decades is not good for a vehicle. This 1970 Plymouth Barracuda had leaves covering it for who knows how long, allowing the moisture to eat away

HILLS OF
MISSOURI

When you have friends around the country, many doors will open for you. Missouri friends said that when I had a spare day, they would show me a Mopar junkyard I would not believe. I took the bait, and arranged to make the trip on New Year's weekend.

I drive my 2009 Dodge Challenger R/T everywhere, and it's great fun except that the final leg of my journey into Missouri farmland was along a snow-covered dirt road. The Challenger made it—barely. Once there, my friends and I walked with the owner for hours. I realized very quickly that my car was, by far, the newest vehicle in the place. Our group went up and down every row, determined to see everything. We would finish with one area, then walk over a hill, and find another field full of cars. We would step into a forest and discover 50 more cars. It was non-stop!

The owner had been drag racing since the cars in his yard were new. Over the years, he had driven against the biggest names in the sport. He showed us his shop, where he had lined the walls with career memorabilia—and these walls were very long and at least 20 feet tall!

Rare 426 Hemi intakes sat in a corner. Nearby were the remains of a race car. Far above our heads, the original Chrysler Pentastar flag from one of the now-closed St. Louis assembly plants hung from the rafters. You could look up, down, and sideways for hours and still miss things.

When we finally stepped from the shop, the owner asked me to look to my left; he said he had to move "a few cars" before a party he was throwing. Well, the "few" turned out to be rows of project cars lined up in a farm field.

Good stuff grows in Missouri.

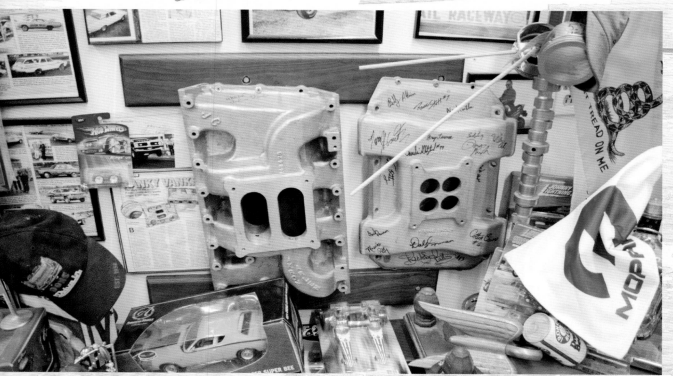

EPIC
JUNKYARD

As I write this, I am 30 years old. I was born well after the original muscle car era. I love these great cars, but there never was a time (especially in Chicago) when I could stroll into a junkyard and find a row of Challengers or Chevelles. Recently, though, I located a yard that blows just about every other one right out of the water. The place has a collection of rare and desirable classic muscle that I had never seen in such numbers.

For me, it started with a story I struggled to believe, a story about row upon row of cool and rare cars sitting derelict in a junkyard. I pieced together some clues and was finally able to track down a name and a location. When I phoned, the owner invited me to look at what he had.

He was a nice guy who had inherited the yard from his father. Early on, the yard gathered "worthless" cars and piled them out back. The present owner didn't sell the cars, he just put them away. And so they've sat, in an open field, for decades.

The yard has a little bit of everything. A 1946 Lincoln Continental convertible was impressive.

I found a 1971 Dodge Challenger R/T 440-6 with a shaker hood still attached and a tree growing through it. The Challenger sat on top of a '69 Dodge Charger R/T. Rare cars were everywhere. I saw two GTO Judges, two 396 SS Novas with engines, and a 1970 AAR 'Cuda! I walked for hours, documenting everything. The experience was exhilarating.

I checked every section of forest, every bush, because there were things so deep in the weeds you had to dig to see them. In my experience, for rarity and quantity, this yard was unique.

Ask questions, meet people, look around. You could be pleasantly surprised.

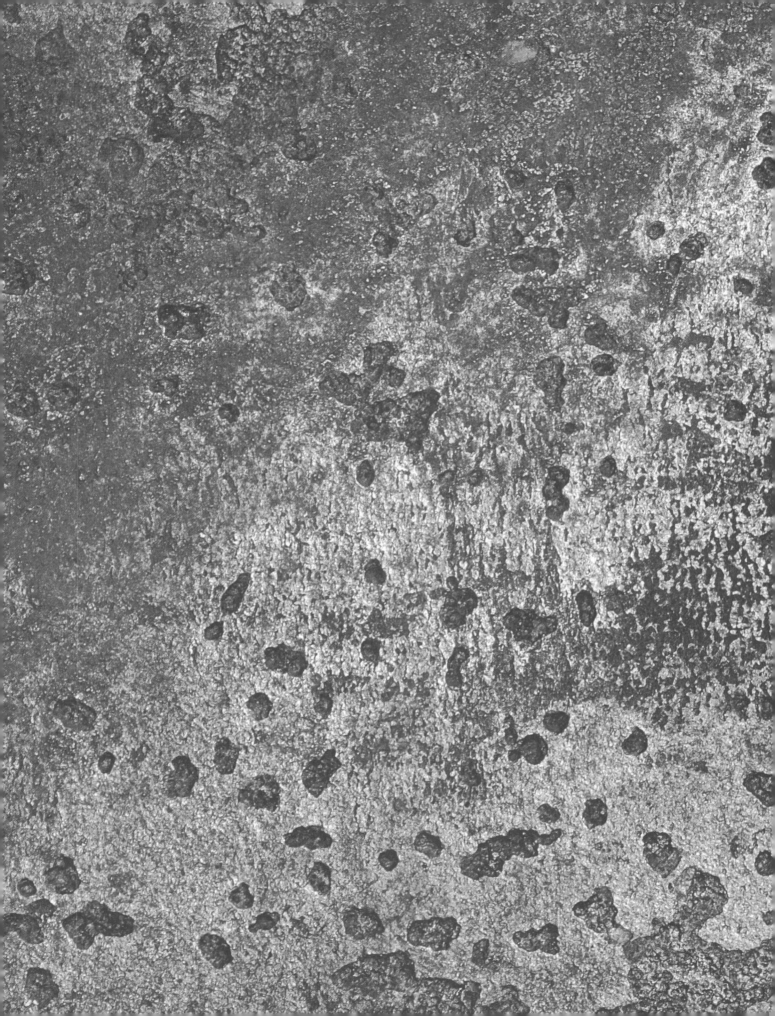